GROWING SPIRITUALLY WITH GOD

CONNECTING WITH MY SPIRIT

TEACHER AND STUDENT WORKBOOK

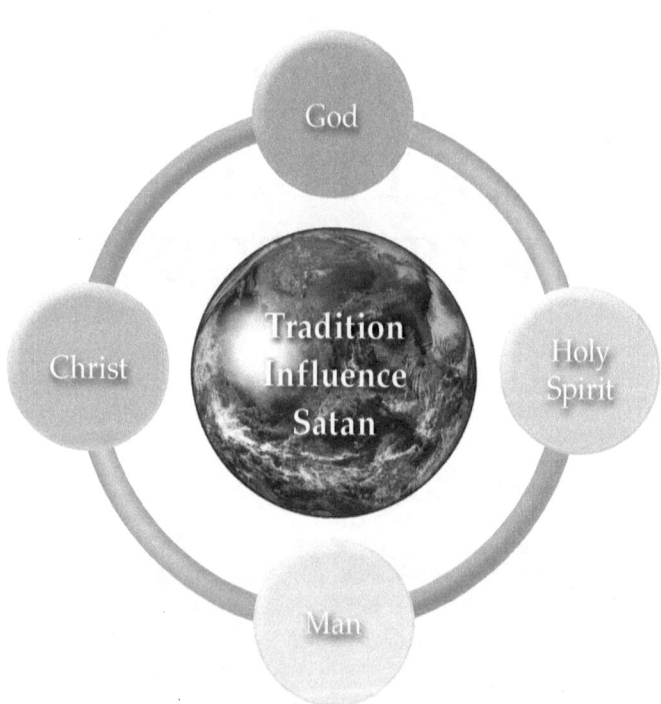

GROWING SPIRITUALLY WITH GOD

CONNECTING WITH MY SPIRIT

TEACHER AND STUDENT WORKBOOK

Frederick L. Coffey

Frederick L Coffey
2015

Copyright © 2015 by Frederick L Coffey

All rights reserved. This book or any portion thereof may not be reproduced or used in any manner whatsoever without the express written permission of the publisher except for the use of brief quotations in a book review or scholarly journal.

First Printing: 2015

ISBN: 978-0-9963288-0-7

Frederick L Coffey
557 Cactus Spur
Killeen, TX 76542

Cover and Interior design: 1106 Design

Library of Congress Control Number: 2015906458

DEDICATION

To my lovely wife, Evette R. Coffey, for sharing her vision of me writing a booklet that would inspire others to seek the basics of Christian faith.

Thank you. Without your support and patience, I never would have achieved my dream.

CONTENTS

Acknowledgments....................................ix

Foreword...xi

Preface..xiii

Introduction.......................................1

Chapter 1: Growing Spiritually With God.............3

Chapter 2: Sexual Integrity 21

Chapter 3: The Holy Spirit and the Anointing 43

Appendix 1...63

Bibliography.......................................73

References...75

ACKNOWLEDGMENTS

WOULD LIKE TO THANK my teachers, my editor and all who have assisted me. Pastor Terry Whitley inspired my continuance in spiritual education. Pastor Terry (deceased in October 2013) is the founder of Grace Christian Center, Killeen, TX. He was a great mentor and spiritual father to me. I also thank Senior Pastor Mark Price. Thanks to Reverend Frederick Rowlett, Pastor at New Testament Baptist Church, Florence, AL; Reverend Brady Butler, House of Life Changing Faith, Florence, AL and Dr. Donald Smith, Antioch Missionary Baptist Church, Tyler, TX, also my spiritual mentor during my practicum of Spiritual Leadership; and, of course, my spouse, Evette Coffey, without whose help this workbook series would never have been completed.

Thank you for your patience and guidance, your use of the editor's red pen… Thanks to all who were instrumental in completing this task.

FOREWORD

THIS STUDY LESSON, "Growing Spiritually with God," has been carefully thought out and led by the Holy Spirit. The lesson is easy for one to understand in Bible study and his/her spiritual walk with God.

Upon studying this lesson, I found the writer to be profound in Biblical doctrine with a burning desire to teach the word of God. The lesson has been designed to help students keep an open mind as they begin their walk with God and become the Role Models that God would have us to be.

I find this lesson would be most effective taught in a group session. This will allow the teacher to answer any questions or concerns that the students may have. May the Lord continue to inspire the writer with His knowledge and wisdom to reach those that are thirsty for God's word.

— Rev. F. C. Rowlett

PREFACE

THE FIRST CHAPTER of the series *Growing Spiritually With God* is intended to identify your ***spiritual gift*** for service. Often times we know individuals only by their gift, and not always by who they really are as a person. It is their option as an individual if they choose to share their private life. However, many people make the mistake of only sharing themselves and not sharing their *gift* given of God. Example: you know celebrities by their talent for acting, or a sports player by his gifted athletic ability, but not by who they are personally. Therefore, we judge them by the gift that we visually see and not the true character of that person.

The personal challenge for all of you engaging in identifying your *spiritual gift* is to learn what your gift is and use that ability in support of the Body of Christ. The subtitle, *"Connecting with my Spirit as to who I am"* is crucial to understanding who you are, and your Gift in Christ that will propel you forward in sharing your gift, and not solely your personal life, as many others often mistakenly do.

One of the most sensitive topics of discussion is Chapter 2, *"Sexual Integrity,"* of a Christian and why it is so important to understand the impact it has on your ministry, personal life and the people that are so close to you. It is imperative that Christians remain focused on the word of God concerning Homosexuality/Lesbianism from the standpoint of God's word, and not what seducing and enticing spirits of this world are introducing into the lives of people, saying it is an acceptable norm of life. Our younger generation will be confused as to what God has really ordained for true marriage and relationship of a man and woman. The Supreme ruling in America, concerning *Same Sex Marriage,* in 2015, has given the approval of both male and female partners to marry within all fifty states. My pastor, Mark Price, spoke a biblical truth one Sunday morning, "If you don't believe in Genesis 1:1 then the rest of the Bible means nothing to you." The very fabric of marriage has been taken away per se rather than preserved. People want the benefits of marriage, but they do not want to acknowledge God in his ordained order. I pray that in generations to come, there are still true believers of Christ, led by the Holy Spirit to provide guidance to our younger generation. What has taken place will become a norm for our society and younger generations. How can man change the structure of an institution that is designed for procreation and ordained by God?

Now, speaking concerning the *"Holy Spirit"* in Chapter 3, there is no need for me to challenge an individual intellect of the *"Holy Spirit"* but ask one simple question: have you truly received the *Holy Spirit,* since you believe? First, the believer must believe and accept the *Holy Ghost* or *Holy Spirit* as the third person in the trinity; and specifically the *Holy Spirit* is identified as a "He" and not an "it" or anything else. In John 14:26, Christ identifies him as a He and the role of the *Holy Spirit* as the Comforter or the Helper in other translations; and the Holy Spirit will teach you all things. The *Holy Spirit* has been involved since the beginning — Genesis 1:1-2.

Throughout the Bible we find there are many illustrations of the Spirit of God working within the framework of God's divine order in creation and man. The Holy Spirit acts only in accordance with the will of God. In the Old Testament scriptures, often we see the Holy Spirit moving upon men for *empowerment* of a specific service or operating in the gift of prophecy. Joseph's dreams were divinely inspired by the working of the Holy Spirit as He moved upon him — Genesis 41:38; and David in 2 Samuel 23:2, prophecy to Israel. In other times, the Spirit of God moves upon men to perform supernatural abilities beyond normal human strength. Judges Chapter 14 tells the familiar story of Samson killing a young lion on his way to Timnah. Verse 6 of that Chapter says "the Spirit of the Lord came mightily upon him." In our lives today, the *Holy Spirit* is dwelling in the believer to empower the supernatural ability of man, to teach and bring back into remembrance what you have heard and taught of Christ.

INTRODUCTION

WANT TO TAKE A MOMENT to introduce to you Part I of a two-part series — *Growing Spiritually With God*. It is very impactful with scriptural support and necessary for enhancing new members' orientation of basic Christian introduction to the Body of Christ, not your church doctrine, but God and Christ. There are specific topics that new members of the Body of Christ should know and feel comfortable in their own spirit as to why a Christian (follower of Christ) believes what they believe. Rarely do spiritual leaders lecture on these topics in their ministry because of scrutiny or fear of the congregation. One important phrase to remember: God is a God of order, structure and authority; and He will not break the integrity of His word to please anyone. The Bible tells us that "Heaven and Earth" will pass away before one "Jot or Tittle" of this word is changed — Mathew 5:18.

This series is designed to open your spiritual eyes to the changes that are affecting the Christian Church through political decision, false doctrinal teachings and increased sensitivity to the moving of God in your life, family and community. To develop a clear understanding of God and purpose we must first return to our original state of being spiritual — *"Connecting With My Spirit As To Who I Am"* to connect with the teachings of God spiritually.

Part II of the series, *Growing Spiritually With God*, will carry you deeper into the understanding of *Prayer & Fasting*. There are different types of *Fasts* and languages of *Prayer*. We deal with the issues of *Spiritual Leadership;* speaking and standing firm against those issues that are contrary to the Word of God. Series II will cover Spiritual Leadership dealing with the issues of divorce, true forgiveness of the heart and restoration back into fellowship with Christ and church. Spiritual Leaders have to know when they are hearing from God and not being influenced by the world. Finally, facing the challenge that many believe is irrelevant to the church and that is giving of *Tithes, Offering and Sacrifices*. Our first impressions of Biblical text or messages are generally through the influence, traditions and opinions of others. This is how we gather and analyze what is being said or what we read, and is being introduced through other men's ideological or theological views.

The objective of both parts of the series is to help develop a strong sense for the word of God, Christ and the Holy Spirit in every aspect of your life.

CHAPTER 1

GROWING SPIRITUALLY WITH GOD

GROWING SPIRITUALLY with God requires individual Christians to look within their own life and seek out those areas where we have not allowed the Spirit of God to manifest Himself. It is through us, by the Spirit, we grow into what God calls us to be. When the Spirit of God manifests Himself through us, this is when we, as Christians, begin to feel or have life-changing experiences with God and Christ. Everything God will do here on earth is through man. You are that instrument of purpose through which God will respond to the needs of His people. Christians will differentiate between the Gifts of the Father, Gifts of the Holy Spirit and the Gifts of Christ unto the Church.

GROWING SPIRITUALLY WITH GOD

PURPOSE: To motivate the saints of God to grow deeper spiritually and to become effective in church, family and in your community. This is not by any means easy but a challenge to being who you are in Christ; and a demonstration in Spirit and of the power of Christ Jesus in your life.

SPEAKERS:
- *Identifying your Gift in God*
- *Identifying who you are in Christ*
- *Growing Spiritually through Prayer and God's Word*
- *You should have at least three things feeding into your "Gift" or "Ministry"*
- *Moving out of your "Comfort Zone" and stepping out in Faith*
- *In what areas of your life do you sense the need for a Divine Healing?*

TALKING POINTS:

Identifying your Gift in God Being effective within your gifted calling is to have an understanding of your "Gift" and how your gift operates within the body of Christ, and within your individual ministry. Our "Gifts" complement each other according to the scripture in I Corinthians 3:6, Paul says, *"I planted, Apollos watered, but God gave the increase"* (KJV). Jesus gives to His Church ministering gifts for the sake of equipping and qualifying Christians for ministry. The gifts profit the church in the sense that they bring together the Body of Christ (believers) in recognition ***of its mutual need of one another*** (I Cor.12:14-26). The intention is not to focus on what gifts of the Spirit we have, but to focus on the fact that we *may be benefited together.* The first point is to recognize *our mutuality of dependence on the grace of God happening through one another.* Ref: Holman Illustrate Bible Dictionary (HIBD)

Scripture: 1 Corinthians 12:8-10
There are different types of Office and Spiritual Gifts within the church _____

_____
_____
_____
_____
_____
_____
_____

Scripture: Romans 12:3-8
Identify what your Gift in Christ is _____

_____
_____
_____
_____
_____
_____

Scripture: I Timothy 4:12; 2 Timothy 1:6-11

Do not neglect using your "Gift" _____

_____
_____
_____
_____
_____

Identifying who you are in Christ Understand who you are and the authority you have in Christ Jesus. Before you can fully operate within your *Gift*, you must receive kingdom power, which is the Holy Spirit. The Holy Spirit is the enabling of your *Gift*. He assists you and gives you the ability to serve others. The Holy Spirit must be "received;" it is not an instinctive experience. Have you received the Holy Spirit since you believe? Acts 19:1-3, it is **imperative** that you operate in your *"Gift"* through the Holy Spirit. This is how you grow spiritually with God, because God is a Spirit.

Scripture: John 7:37-38, Acts 1:4-8, Ephesians 1:11, Ephesians 1:13

You are chosen (predestined) by God for service. _____

_____
_____
_____
_____

be unwavering in studying the word of God. Growing spiritually literally means becoming knowledgeable of God's word, developing a deeper understanding of Christ and the teachings of the Holy Spirit to be effective in your ministry. Paul said in 1 Corinthians 2:1-5 *"And I, brethren, when I came to you, came not with excellency of speech or of wisdom, declaring unto you the testimony of God. For I determined not to know anything among you, save Jesus Christ, and him crucified. And I was with you in weakness, and in fear, and in much trembling. And my speech and my preaching was not with enticing words of man's wisdom, but in demonstration of the Spirit and of power: That your faith should not stand in the wisdom of men, but in the power of God."* (KJV)

Scripture: 2 Timothy 2:15, 2 Peter 3:18

Study to show yourself ready and available for ministry, not to man but unto God. _____

_____
_____
_____
_____
_____
_____

Scripture: Romans 8:26-27; 2 Peter 1:5-8

Prayer is your communication unto God. The Spirit must intercede because our prayers are weak; apart from the Spirit, Christians pray without discernment. He, *Holy Spirit,* takes up our petitions with an earnest pleading beyond words.

Scripture: Matthew 26:38-39, 42, 45; Paul in 2 Corinthians 12:8-9

Not every petition, every prayer, is granted. Do not become discouraged when God does not grant you your request.

You should have at least three things feeding into your "Gift" or "Ministry." You as an individual Christian do not have all the answers. You have to face the fact that you are limited. Therefore, you should have at least three sources feeding into your ministry and spiritual growth. Consistently, the word of God should always be the primary thing on your list feeding into your spiritual life. Secondly, prayer is important; however, it is not enough, because you need a physical connection to exchange thoughts, ideas and knowledge to meet certain needs. Thirdly, a mentor who is serious about your spiritual growth and well-being. It would be a good practice to have someone above your level of thinking to become your "mentor."

Scripture: Romans 8:1-9

Being Spiritual and living a spiritual life. You live in a carnal world but your response should be spiritual.

Scripture: John 4:24

Christians need a truthful worship lifestyle to grow spiritually in God.

GROWING SPIRITUALLY WITH GOD

Scripture: Luke 10:1-20 Christ sent out the seventy two-by-two; and they returned with an encouraging report.

Christians need a "Mentor" in their life to help guide them along the way.

- Prayer
- Holy Spirit
- Mentor

Moving out of your "Comfort Zone" and stepping out in Faith This is one of the most difficult challenges Christians will confront within themselves; stepping out of their personal "Comfort Zone" to perform the work God has chosen for you. The disciples left what they had to follow Christ. Often times, we think our life has a certain pattern which we must follow. However, God will disrupt your life and plans for His agenda. If you are called by God and chosen for a particular ministry, then you probably have experienced God moving you into another direction than originally planned. Are you afraid to move forward because of what people might say or think about you? Growing Spiritually with God is stepping out in-faith with what God has placed in your spirit.

Scripture: Acts 13:2

"As they ministered to the Lord and fasted, the Holy Spirit said, Now separate to Me Barnabas and Saul for the work to which I have called them."

Are you afraid to move forward into what God has called you into? _____

_____

_____

_____

_____

_____

_____

Scripture: Hebrews 11:1

"Now faith is the substance of things hoped for, the evidence of things not seen. For by it the elders obtained a good testimony. By faith we understand that the worlds were framed by the word of God, so that the things which are seen were not made of things which are visible."

How strong is your faith in believing in your ministry?

Scripture: Matthew 17:20, 2 Timothy 1:7.

What challenges are you confronting that hinder you from moving forward?

In what areas in your life do you sense the need for a Divine Healing? What specific points do you see as needful of "Recovery" or "Restoration" in your life? David had to be restored with God through Nathan, the prophet, because of his adulterous spirit that caused him to commit adultery with Bathsheba; and have her husband Uriah placed in the forefront of the "hottest battle" to be killed, 2 Samuel Chapters 11 and 12.

Scripture: 2 Samuel Chapters 11 & 12.

Identify the areas in your life needing healing; that which can prevent you from serving God faithfully. _____

_____

_____

_____

_____

_____

Scripture: Galatians 6:1; Col 3:13.

Restoring that which was lost…or restore others in Christ that have fallen. _____

_____

_____

_____

_____

Scripture: 2 Corinthians 2:7-10.

Is it difficult for you to forgive? It is not an option. Jesus places enormous emphasis on horizontal (human to human) forgiveness. Because Christians have been redeemed, they are obligated to forgive as they have been forgiven.

CONCLUSION:

Ministering to people (souls) is the purpose of your calling in Christ. Your gift makes room for you in an environment that is thirsty and hungry for righteousness. If those who are called are not leading the charge, God can and possibly will choose others to perform His will. I don't think any of us really want a Jonah experience, but perhaps this may be what it takes to actively move you forward in Christ. The idea and purpose of this session is to enhance your Spiritual Life with God and become an active Christian in your community, family and church to make a difference through illustration (your life).

- How do pride, selfishness, self-deception and wrong motives combine with our personality and life experiences to hinder your spiritual growth with God and Christ?

- What are the signs of its presence in your life, attitude, behavior and leadership that you have not addressed?

It is these important questions that we have not answered within ourselves. It is impossible to help others grow or grow spiritually without correcting these issues in your life. It is not the past that defines a "man" or "woman;" it is what he/she does with their past to better their future, to change the course of their life through God and Christ, for their family and those with whom they come into contact with.

- God
- Christ
- Holy Spirit
- Body
- Spirit
- Soul

There are things which you must do to become spiritually sound, just as an athlete trains to become a professional at what he/she desires. You have to build up every side of you for the glory of the ministry through prayer, studying and being in good health.

A person exercises to build his/her body with the hope of being healthy. You read the Bible to build up your mind, and you pray to strengthen your spirit. The Third Epistle of John vs 2 says, *"Beloved, I pray that you may prosper in all things and be in health, just as your soul prospers."*

- You can have a strong body and be thoughtless if you don't read or pray.

- You can have knowledge and spiritual insight, but if the body is weak and sick all the time, you can't be used for service.

- You can have a strong body and wisdom, but if you don't have a prayer life, how can you lead God's people spiritually?

Christians seek to grow spiritually with God. Growing with God may require you to forsake those around you; and sometimes, this may mean family members or relatives. As hard as this may sound, it is true for *"Spiritual Growth."* Jesus says to us in Luke 18:29, *"And he said unto them, Verily I say unto you, There is no man that hath left house, or parents, or brethren, or wife, or children, for the kingdom of God's sake,"* (KJV). Even in your own household, you will experience enemies for the sake of the gospel to obtain a deeper relationship with God and Christ.

It's difficult to make such decisions because we are attached to and love those around us; and God is calling you or has called you to separate yourself to the ministry in which He has ordained for you.

Detach yourself from negative influences.

Remove yourself from false teachings.
Stop feeding off the *"Milk of the Word."* It's time to dig deeper into studying and the Holy Ghost is waiting to take you there. The Holy Spirit *teaches* and gives *Wisdom.*

In I Corinthians 3:2, Paul speaks to the people about growing spiritually and again in Hebrews 5:12-14.

In order to properly grow spiritually, we must spend quality time in word and separate ourselves from hindrances, negative influences, competitive spirit in the church and a host of other things.

At some point, you recognized the call of God in your life. There is a difference between being a *"Man of God"* and *"God's Man":* the latter is a call to leadership. Many are called **sovereignly** by God. Examples are:

Moses — through the burning bush Moses heard God speak to him, Exodus 3:1-4; 17.

The Prophet Samuel was called while he was asleep, I Samuel 3:1-18. What's so interesting about his calling was that Samuel *did not know the voice* of God. Eli, the prophet, had to instruct him. In 1 Samuel 3:9 it says *"Therefore Eli said unto Samuel, Go, lie down: and it shall be, if he call thee, that thou shalt say,* **Speak, LORD; for thy servant heareth.** *So Samuel went and lay down in his place."*

The Prophet Isaiah — was worshipping in the temple when called by God, Isaiah 6:1-9.

The Prophet Jeremiah — was called by God. God's sovereignty is shown in that He formed, sanctified *(set apart),* and ordained *(appointed)* to be a prophet 1:1-5; 9-12. Verse number 11 is an important verse I would like to point out. Jeremiah 1:11 *"Moreover the word of the LORD came unto me, saying, Jeremiah,* **what seest thou?** *And I said, I see a rod of an almond tree. Then said the LORD unto me,* **Thou hast well seen:** *for I will hasten my word to perform it."* (KJV). Are you seeing or interpreting the word of God correctly? Ask yourself this question, am I questioning the vision God has manifested?

Here are a few points to remember:

Listen to the voice of God
- Remove distraction
- Turn of the TV & Music

Develop a personal worship time
- Pray earnestly to God
- Develop a life of Fasting

Develop regular study habits
- Consecrate yourself unto God
- Are you seeing the vision clearly?

CHAPTER 2

SEXUAL INTEGRITY

THE MOST VULNERABLE people, I think, to be attacked by Satan, are Spiritual Leaders and those who faithfully serve God. What God had intended for the good of man's relationship between a man and a woman, Satan has used against man's lustful desires of the flesh; and so likewise the woman as well. It is one of the most tempting desires that each person has in common: intimacy with another person. There are Christians who live as faithfully as they know how; and struggle with unhealthy desires in their lives, and face the challenges of a renewing mind in Christ Jesus. People want the benefits of God's structured marriage and relationship; however, they refuse to acknowledge or accept God's principles and ordained order for the union of a man and woman. The most recent ruling from the Supreme Court of America, will affect the institution of marriage created and ordained by God. Our younger generation in years to come will believe it is normal and acceptable for same sex individuals to be married and a norm to have same sex couples as parents. Now, we have the potential, of having same sex couples adopting children.

PURPOSE: Recognizing the addictions in your life. It may not necessarily be Sexual, but there may be an addiction just as tempting and dangerous to yourself and others; and too embarrassing to share publicly. Defeating Satan over the carnal flesh can only be achieved by acknowledging and confessing the problem; and only through spiritual warfare can you defeat the war between flesh and spirit.

SPEAKERS:
- *What is True Christian Integrity (Women).*
- *Understanding a Sin against your Body is a Sin against Christ.*
- *Controlling the Sexual desires of the flesh.*
- *Homosexuals/Lesbianism tendencies are against God's nature.*
- *What is True Christian Integrity (Men).*
- *Integrity of the heart toward God, Christ and the Holy Spirit.*
- *Preventing erosion of Christian Integrity "It destroys one's Life and Character" and develops false character.*
- *How does Integrity work in the Human Personality?*
- *The works of the flesh are divided into four categories in Galatians 5:19-21.*

- *Four primary Sexual Sins the Word of God specifically addresses.*

TALKING POINTS:

What is True Christian Integrity (Women)? True Integrity is living a life before Christ that reflects who you really are as a Christian before the world publicly. When you think of *Integrity*, it is the consistency of your character, ethics, and personal commitment to values and principles you have accepted from God, Christ and the Holy Spirit present in your life. Integrity is only perfect in the absence of its teacher; and demonstrated openly to the highest standards of respect. You are uncompromising and stand in opposition of hypocrisy.

Scripture: Ps. 7:8; 101:2; Job 2:3; and 1 Kings 9:4

In Genesis 20:3-7, God speaks to Abimelech in a dream about Abraham's wife, Sarah. *"But God came to Abimelech in a dream by night, and said to him, Behold, thou art but a dead man, for the woman which thou hast taken; for she is a man's wife. But Abimelech had not come near her: and he said, Lord, wilt thou slay also a righteous nation? Said he not unto me, She is my sister? And she, even she herself said, He is my brother: in the integrity of my heart and innocence of my hands have I done this. And God said unto him in a dream, Yea, I know that thou didst this in the integrity of thy heart; for I also withheld thee from sinning against me: therefore suffered I thee not to touch her. Now therefore restore the man his wife; for he is a prophet, and he shall pray for thee, and thou shalt live: and if thou restore her not, know thou that thou shalt surely die, thou, and all that are thine."* (KJV).

What issues of *Integrity* are you personally confronting presently in your spiritual walk with God? _____

_____
_____
_____
_____
_____
_____
_____
_____

Scripture: Matthew 12:43-45

Are there any past *Integrity* desires that keep pressing their way to resurface within your life? If so, there is the potential that Satan is trying to reenter your life. _____

_____
_____
_____
_____
_____
_____
_____

SEXUAL INTEGRITY 25

Understanding a Sin against your Body is a Sin against Christ When a person becomes saved, the challenge we have as Christian brothers and sisters in Christ, is teaching others how to live a life holy and acceptable unto God, away from what the world thinks holy is.

Scripture: 1 Corinthians 6:15; 19-20; Romans 12:1

Are you as a Christian presenting your life and body as a temple for the indwelling of the Holy Spirit? _____

Scripture: 1 Corinthians 1:11, 1 Corinthians 5:1.

Dealing with the deeds of the flesh. _____

Scripture: Exodus 20:19; Lev 18:6-18, 22-23.

Controlling the Sexual Desires of the Flesh As Christians you have to allow the Holy Spirit to guide every aspect of your life. You will continue to struggle with flesh until you surrender your heart completely to Christ. By the renewing of your mind, you can change the effects of the flesh by submitting to the word of God.

Scripture: 1 Corinthians 9:24-27; 2 Peter 1:6; Galatians 5:22-23; Matthew 5:28.

Self-control is expressed through the fruits of the Spirit. When Christians struggle with the flesh as identified in Galatians 5:16-17, then there are specific (spirits) actions that can or will express itself through your flesh.

Homosexuality/Lesbianism is against God's nature and divine order Sexual immorality is in direct conflict with procreation; however, it is natural for humanity to have a sexual drive for the opposite sex, but it is dangerous if it is not kept in its proper perspective within God's instruction. The ideology of the world's views on intimacy, between man and woman, does not necessarily cover God's instruction nor His wisdom or knowledge in biblical teachings. Our culture has embraced such behavior as a norm; and as an acceptable way to live sociably; and acknowledges this union between man/man and woman/woman, as part of life. It is very apparent that the story of Sodom and Gomorrah (Genesis Chapters 18–19) has no effect upon present day people living ungodly. Spirits actually attach themselves to humans to act out who they are. Spirits are disembodied beings (will be covered in another section). What man cannot explain, they describe as a chemical imbalance; however, the Bible deals with man's conditions as a spirit.

Scripture: Roman 1:21-22, 26-27; Genesis Chapter 18 and 19; Lev 18:16-18, 22-23.

How are you dealing with spirits of homosexuality/lesbianism within your family, church, work environment or perhaps a friend? _____

_____

_____

_____

_____

_____

_____

Scriptures: 1 Corinthians 5:1-13.

Spiritual Leaders have fallen short in teaching concerning incest and other sexual misconduct in fear of what the congregations might say or do. Dealing with *"Sexual Deviance"* in the church is not a delicate subject. Paul spoke of the church misconduct in I Cor. 5:1-13. _____

_____

_____

_____

_____

_____

Scripture: Romans 1:18-32; 1 Timothy 4:1-2, Proverbs 6:28.

There is a great falling away from the faith of Christ, and worshipping the Living God. Seducing spirits and demons have influenced people to worship their body. Some Christians have become insensitive to the Spirit of God, just as the scripture says in 1 Timothy 4:1-2 and Pr. 6:28.

What is True Christian Integrity (Men)? *Integrity* is complete wholeness of *"Heart"* before God, Christ and the Holy Spirit. In 1 Thessalonians 5:19 says *"Quench not the Spirit"* (KJV) so we must be careful not to quench the Holy Spirit, by indulging carnal lusts and affections and minding only earthly things. Ephesians 4:30, *"And do not grieve the Holy Spirit of God, by whom you were sealed for the day of redemption."* (KJV). Sometimes we live in a world of our own that is a **"deceptive supposition"**: because you are surrounded by righteousness, they would automatically be righteous. This is false deception of one's self-internal spirit. When Christians **"violate fundamental principles"** and not that of just simply morality, they also **violate fundamental principles** of *Integrity*. Christians know what they are doing or engaging in is wrong and violate their own hearts before God. Just as David did when he lusted after Bathsheba. The heart of this discussion is about *Integrity*.

Scripture: Psalm 7:8, 25:21, 41:12, 78:72; Proverbs 10:9, Titus 2:7.

Jack Hayford, a well-renowned man of God, says this about Integrity *"The key to your growth, your fruitfulness and your fulfillment in Jesus Christ — in life as a human being — is integrity of heart. The key to growth is not the Bible; it's not studying the Word of God. That is a key to growth, and you cannot grow without the Word of God, but that is not the key. There are many people who study the Word of God that do not have a heart for God.* **Integrity has to do with a heart for God.**"

Scripture: Ezekiel 3:10; Mark 7:6-23; Acts 5:3; 2 Corinthians 3:3.

You are dealing with more than just your personal feelings of the heart; you are interacting with God's ordained order for man's internal spirit that is the stewardship of your personality. Your conscience can become insensitive to God's word. Integrity is that which keeps the heart in line with God's word. You will become sensitive and responsive to

His spirit and word. It is absolute honesty with God and yourself, without the presence of anyone else.

Integrity of the heart toward God, Christ and the Holy Spirit There are many things that can cause a Christian to become insensitive to the Spirit of God and cause him/her to lose focus in maintaining *Integrity*. The challenges you face are real and true; and you are the only one standing between them and your integrity before God. Consider the Abimelech and Joseph and what they had to endure. Their situations were real, but they upheld the word of God in their hearts and because they did so, God spared Abimelech and whatever Joseph did, the Lord made it prosper. It is the *Integrity* of your heart when you are not being watched.

Scripture: Genesis 20, Abimelech demonstrated integrity and Joseph Genesis 39.

Joseph also demonstrated *Integrity* before God while a servant in Potiphar House. However, Joseph's *Integrity* was tested by Potiphar's wife.

Scripture: David's prayer in Psalm 139.

One of the most imperative keys for Christian spiritual growth is *Integrity* of heart. It's the key to our fruitfulness, the key to our advancement, and the key to being protected from ourselves. It's the key protecting you from yourself. Christians must listen to the voice of their heart quickened by the Lord. _____

_____

_____

_____

_____

_____

_____

_____

_____

Preventing erosion of Christian Integrity — "it destroys one Life and Character" and develops false character:

**Scripture: Numbers Chapter 22-24;
Proverbs 2:6-8; Romans 12:1-2.**

These chapters in the book of Numbers provide a great illustration of Balaam standing fast in his *Integrity* before God. No matter what the offer was from Balak, he remained focused on what God has instructed in his heart concerning the people of Israel. Balaam says this to Balak in Numbers 24:12-13 (KJV). *"And Balaam said unto Balak, Spake I not also to thy messengers which thou sentest unto me, saying, If Balak would give me his house full of silver and gold, I cannot go beyond the commandment of the LORD, to do either good or bad of mine own mind; but what the LORD saith, that will I speak?"*

Scripture: Acts 5:1-11 Ananias and Sapphira, Psalms 1:1-2.

As Christians, you cannot covet the wealth of the world, and be distrustful to God and His providence. Christians sometimes think they can deceive the shepherd, but the Spirit of God will reveal to His shepherd the falseness of one's heart.

_____

_____

_____

How does Integrity work in the Human Personality? David says in Psalm 119:11 *"Thy word have I hid in my heart, that I might not sin against thee."* *Integrity* is the inner intermediary of the heart. Christians, no doubt, have to practice *Integrity* of the heart. It is what tells you *yea* or *nay* to something you're thinking. *Integrity* will preserve you. There are many professing spirituality but not living the life that reflects Christ's principles. God looks at the heart of man whereas we can only see the outward appearance of a man, but not the truthfulness of his heart. Christ lived the life of perfect *Integrity of Heart* before God and illustrated to man how to deal with various temptations in life.

Scripture: Job 2:3, 2:9, 27:5; Titus 2:7-8.

Christian Quotes:

"Integrity is keeping a commitment even after circumstances have changed."

~ David Jeremiah

"Integrity is built by defeating the temptation to be dishonest; humility grows when we refuse to be prideful; and endurance develops every time you reject the temptation to give up."

~ Rick Warren

SEXUAL INTEGRITY 35

> *"We must be the same person in private and in public. Only the Christian worldview gives us the basis for this kind of integrity."*
> ~ Chuck Colson

The works of the flesh are divided into four Categories in Galatians 5:19-21 There are at least four primary sexual sins the Word of God speaks of: adultery, fornication, uncleanness and lewdness. Here are the definitions of these four sexual sins: **Adultery:** Unlawful sexual intercourse involving at least one married person. Adultery is incompatible with the harmonious laws of family life in God's kingdom, and is under God's judgment since it violates God's original purpose. **Fornication:** Pornography, illicit sexual intercourse including prostitution, whoredom, incest, licentiousness (lack of moral restraint), and habitual immorality (including sexual fantasies that lead to masturbation). **Uncleanness:** Often refers to homosexuality and lesbianism. **Lewdness:** unashamed indecency, unbridled lust, unrestrained depravity (a disposition or settled tendency to evil; the innate corruption of unregenerate man). The person with this characteristic has an insolent defiance of public opinion, sinning in broad daylight with arrogance and contempt.   Ref: Holman Illustrated Bible Dictionary

Scripture: Matthew 15:19; Galatians 5:19-21, 1 Corinthians 5:1-6, 6:9-20; Ephesians 5:3-20; Colossians 3:5; 1 Thessalonians 4:1-5.

At the moment, it is very critical that we understand the word of God and the impact of our exciting society's views and interpretation of the scriptures. Cultures around the world have accepted lifestyles such as homosexuality/lesbianism as a norm. When we separate ourselves from the true Living God, seducing spirits enter into our lives and draw us from the Spirit of God. It is so important that you understand God and have a relationship with Christ. It is more than just going to Bible study and church on Sunday; it is having a deeper journey in your life with God and listening to the spirit that is speaking truth to your soul.

___

Dealing with the unexpected that arises in your life is challenging. You will encounter the unexpected in your life that will desperately try to influence you into partaking of things unhealthy for *Spiritual Growth*. In particular, I am speaking of *seducing spirits* that walk through dry places seeking a place to live out their *Sexual Sinful* nature of immorality.

Four primary Sexual Sins the Word of God specifically addresses. The Bible specifically covers the Sexual Sins that are against the true nature of God. What's so interesting is that people want God-ordained principles for marriage and relationship without commitment and accountability to God or the required lifestyle of a Christian. The specific four *"Sexual Sins"* can be referred to as: Adultery, Fornication, Uncleanliness and Lewdness from Galatians 5:19.

What is Adultery? An act of unfaithfulness in marriage that occurs when one of the marriage partners voluntarily engages in sexual intercourse with a person other than the marriage partner. Exodus 20:14; Matthew 15:19; and lust is as much a violation of the law's intent as is illicit sexual intercourse (Matt. 5:27-28). Adultery is one of the "works of the flesh" (Gal. 5:19). It creates enmity with God (James 4:4), and adulterers will not inherit the kingdom of God (1 Cor. 6:9). Adulterers can be forgiven (John 8:3-11); and once sanctified through repentance, faith, and God's grace, they are included among God's people (1 Cor. 6:9-11).

What is Fornication? Various acts of sexual immorality, especially being a harlot or whore. Paul extended the use of the Greek term for fornication to cover all sinful sexual activity. He dealt with the problem particularly in writing the Corinthians who faced a society permeated with sexual religion and the sexual sins of a seaport. A believer must decide to be part of Christ's body or a prostitute's body (1 Cor. 6:12-20). The believer must flee sexual immorality and cleave to Christ, honoring Him with the physical body. Fornication is thus a result of sinful human nature (Gal. 5:19) and unsuitable for God's holy people (Eph. 5:3; 1 Thess. 4:3). _____

What is Uncleanliness? Whatever is opposite to purity; as in Romans 1:24; 2 Corinthians 12:21, unnatural practices; sodomy, bestiality. _____

SEXUAL INTEGRITY 39

What is Lewdness? Lust; sexual nonchastity; licentiousness. Lewdness sometimes refers to an especially heinous crime: brutal gang rape resulting in murder (Judg. 19:25-27); unbridled expression of sexual urges (Mark 7:22; 2 Cor. 12:21; Gal. 5:19; Eph. 4:19; 1 Pet. 4:3; Jude 4).

Conclusion/Summary:

All of us will face the issue of *Integrity* in our life. Integrity of the heart toward *God, Christ* and The *Holy Spirit* in the absence of others is very important because it demonstrates your ability to manage self-control over the flesh. The Bible tells us the Spirit of man is willing, but the Flesh of man is weak. Christ tells His disciples in Matthew 26:41 *"Watch and pray that you enter not into temptation: the spirit is indeed willing, but the flesh is weak."* If you can gain control of the flesh (your emotions and feelings) you have won half the battle.

The world has influenced the church on so many levels that it is unbelievable what we have allowed to become a norm for the church. When you separate yourself, or collectively, from God then the spirits of this world will become a major influence in leading you and others from Christ. The seducing spirits of this world are crafty in not telling the full truth; therefore, it is each individual's responsibility to discern and ask questions about things that are unclear. Matthew 24:24 *"For false messiahs and false prophets will appear and perform great signs and wonders to deceive, if possible, even the elect."* When Christians neglect their own personal devotion to study, they are subject to subtle deceit.

The focus is Sexual Integrity and Integrity of the individual. The ideology of the world is to sample things before committing to having it. The author of deceit is Satan himself and has distorted the minds of those who rejected Christ. 2 Corinthians 11:14 *"And no wonder, Even Satan disguises (or masquerades) himself as an angel of light."* The illusion Satan has presented appears to be so Christian-like, that you cannot differentiate between the *Truth* and *Lie*.

From the beginning in Leviticus 18:22, 20:13, God said not to have sexual relations with a man as with a woman and vice versa for the women. Satan has influenced people for years and suggested that worshipping various "Sex Gods" was a natural norm of life. This is why God insisted that Christian spiritual leaders and teachers of His word be prepared to define and show that these spirits are real and not a chemical imbalance. God has warned His people neither to worship nor bow down to any other god. As in the Biblical days, today people still worship false gods such as Baal and Ashtoreth (or Astarte) which were known as fertility gods. The Canaanite people worshipped these gods making sacrifices of humans and performing sexual prostitution in temples to these false gods. Baal was also known during the time of Moses in tribes called the Moabites and the Midinites, which were a negative influence on the people of Israel. Baal is also known as Beelzebub, a fallen angel of Satan. Sexual perversion has been around for a long time and it is here to stay until those spirits have been cast into the pits of hell. I cannot find anywhere listed in the Bible that mentions chemical imbalance to explain the works of evil spirits in people. The author of confusion is Satan.

CHAPTER 3

THE HOLY SPIRIT AND THE ANOINTING

T HE HOLY SPIRIT (often referred to as the *Holy Ghost*) has specific functions within all of us to assist with the delivery of the word of God, ministry specifics and spiritual gifts. Specifically, it equips us with the *Empowerment* or supernatural abilities to perform beyond the very nature of human ability. The principal purpose of the Holy Spirit is to accomplish two unquestionable acts within the lives of Christian believers and that is first, be indwelling and speak what He has heard the Father speak. John 14:25-27 says this specifically: *"All this I have spoken while still with you. But the Advocate, the Holy Spirit, whom the Father will send in my name, will teach you all things and will remind you of everything I have said to you. Peace I leave with you; my peace I give you. I do not give* to you as the world gives. Do not let your hearts be troubled and do not be afraid" (NIV). Is the church seeking CEO mentality or Spiritual-Led Leaders in whom the Spirit of God is indwelling and leading spiritually?

PURPOSE: The objective of this teaching is to rededicate our ministry back into the *Empowerment* of the *Holy Ghost*. Not just becoming a speaker, a story-teller or eloquent presenter, but an effective man and woman of God with a message with purpose and movement upon the hearts of people to change. When preaching, teaching or expounding upon the Gospel of Jesus Christ, it is not by human natural ability, but by the inspiration of the *Holy Spirit* indwelling in the Christian. You're not Clark Kent, who changes into Superman whenever he likes, nor do you turn off the *Holy Spirit* whenever you like to be something different than what God has called you to purposely fulfill in your life. The spirit of Christ lives continuously within the Christians to perform the *Will of God* through you.

SPEAKERS:

- *Is there a difference between the Anointing and the Holy Spirit (Holy Ghost)?*
- *True Preaching or Teaching is demonstrated by the Holy Spirit within you.*
- *Your ministry has to be in line with the Holy Spirit and not a personal agenda.*
- *How do we end up with Spirit Empowerment preaching or teaching, and if this is a question of the heart, then how do I arrive at that destination within my life or ministry?*

- *Preachers and teachers at all times should be Spirit-Led in their messages and not randomly preaching. God comes to His people with a purpose, therefore, the teacher should present with a purpose in mind.*
- *What are the characteristics of being Spirit Empowered (having Authority)?*
- *Have you truly received the Gift of the Father the "Holy Ghost" since you believe?*
- *What role or purpose does the Holy Spirit have in the life of a believer?*

TALKING POINTS:

Is there a difference between the Anointing and the Holy Spirit (Holy Ghost)? One of the most difficult things to teach to Christians is the understanding of the difference between the *Anointing* and the *Holy Spirit*. There is a difference and the objective here is to hopefully give you a clear understanding of what the *Anointing* is and what the *Spirit* is. My gift from God is nothing until the Anointing comes upon me and anoints the gift. You can be gifted and have no anointing behind your gift to impact others. Christ said this very plainly in Luke 4:18 *"The Spirit of the Lord is upon me, because He has anointed me to proclaim good news to the poor"* (NIV). The anointing is the *Power* that flows from the *Holy Spirit*. You can be filled with the spirit, but until you acknowledge what is within you, then the gift will not manifest or come alive.

Paul, 2 Tim. 2:6, tells Timothy to stir up the "Gift" of God that is within Him. Isaiah 10:27, the anointing breaks the yoke, Isaiah 61:1, **anointed me.** 2 Cor.1:21, Acts 10:38.

First John speaks of the anointing of God as the Holy Spirit within a person. I John 2:26-27 *"I am writing these things to you about those who are trying to lead you astray. As for you, the anointing you received from him remains in you, and you do not need anyone to teach you. But as his anointing teaches you about all things and as that anointing is real, not counterfeit — just as it has taught you, remain in him"* (NIV). The Holy Spirit is a person and Christ says so in John 16:7-15.

True Preaching or Teaching is demonstrated by the Holy Spirit within you. How do we actually identify or proclaim true *preaching* or *teaching* of God's word? Paul made a statement very clear to the Christians in 1 Corinthians 2:4-5. *"And my speech and my preaching were not in persuasive words of wisdom, but in demonstration of the Spirit and of power: that your faith stand not in the wisdom of men, but in the power of God"* (ASV). When you are driven by the Spirit of God, then your preaching or teaching is impacted by the *Holy Spirit* working your gifted ability to speak influentially and persuasively.

Becoming a Preacher or Teacher of the word of God, first, you have to truly acknowledge that you were chosen by God to be in such an office. No one can answer your specific call to ministry except you. Some of us were destined before birth and ordained by God. Jeremiah 1:4-5. *"Now the word of Jehovah came unto me, saying, Before I formed thee in the belly I knew thee, and before thou camest forth out of the womb I sanctified thee; I have appointed thee a prophet unto the nations"* (ASV). Being called into the ministry is a call to

"Holiness and *Sanctification."* Being set apart for a specific service for God.

Christ informed His disciples that the Holy Spirit will guide you into all truth. John 16:13 "¹³ *Howbeit when he, the Spirit of truth, is come, he shall guide you into all the truth: for he shall not speak from himself; but what things so ever he shall hear, these shall he speak: and he shall declare unto you the things that are to come"* (ASV). The Holy Spirit is indwelling in the believer, 2 Timothy 2:14, and 1 Corinthians 3:16-17. Spiritual things are spiritually discerned by the *Holy Spirit* and they are foolish to the natural man. The interpretation of scripture is not of man nor of self, but by the *Holy Spirit*. 2 Peter 1:20.

_____

_____

_____

Your ministry has to be in line with the Holy Spirit and not a personal agenda. The *Holy Spirit* works within our Christian lives to perform the works of the ministry in which God has ordained for you. One of the primary reasons our ministries are "**NOT**" effective and powerful today is because Christians do "**NOT**" allow the full operation of the *Holy Ghost* in their life. The church cannot have a separate agenda from that of God's Word. Christ is the ultimate teacher and example of adhering to the will and work of the Father. John 4:32-34 "³² But he said unto them, I have meat to eat that ye know not. ³³ The disciples therefore said one to another, Hath any man brought him *aught to eat?* ³⁴ Jesus *saith unto them, My meat is to do the will of him that sent me, and to accomplish his work*" (ASV). Therefore, your purpose should be in line with the *Will of God* for your ministry. Proverbs 19:21, Isaiah 46:10, John 14:13 and Acts 17:28. Christ says "greater work" John 14:12-14.

Christ provides another specific reason for His ministry. John 6:38-40 "³⁸ *For I am come down from heaven, not to do mine own will, but the will of him that sent me.* ³⁹ *And this is the will of him that sent me, that of all that which he hath given me I should lose nothing, but should raise it up at the last day.* ⁴⁰ *For this is the will of my Father, that every one that beholdeth the Son, and believeth in him, should have eternal life; and I will raise*

THE HOLY SPIRIT AND THE ANOINTING 49

him up at the last day" (ASV). The question to ask yourself is does the ministry (work) God has given you have the right focus? If your church is not growing, then perhaps your ministry is not Spiritually-Led. The work which you are doing should be prospering or your gift should benefit or support the ministry you are under. Christ gave a commandment to the church, a specific work written in Matthew 28:19-20 and *that is to make disciples of all nations.*

If you have a personal hidden agenda that is contrary to the work which God has ordained, then the ministry will not prevail. Christians cannot be influenced by the world in leading spiritually. There are principles and values we can learn; however, it is the *Holy Spirit* that teaches the things of God for spiritual growth. There is no other foundation than the foundation of Christ for ministry. 1 Corinthians 3:13 *"¹³ Each man's work shall be made manifest: for the day shall declare it, because it is revealed in fire; and the fire itself shall prove each man's work of what sort it is"* (ASV).

How do we end up with Spirit Empowerment preaching or teaching, and if this is a question of the heart, then how do I arrive at that destination within my life or ministry? Spirit Empowerment preaching (or Anointing) only comes through diligently studying, praying, fasting and seeking God for the message for His people. This does not exclude the man or woman from developing a series of topical messages which are very helpful and purposeful. Although, the *Holy Spirit* led the Christians to a more purposeful message for a purposeful time to be spoken. In Luke 4:1-2, Matthew 4:1-11, Mark 1:12-13, the *Holy Spirit* led Christ and prepared Him for what is to come. The growth of your ministry depends upon your ability to be sensitive to the spirit movement and not sensual but sensitive to hearing the spirit speak.

The Empowerment (or Anointing) comes by the indwelling of the Holy Spirit and living a life that reflects the character of Christ. Romans 12:1-2, 1 Corinthians 3:16-17 *"16 Know ye not that ye are a temple of God, and that the Spirit of God dwelleth in you? 17 If any man destroyeth the temple of*

God, him shall God destroy; for the temple of God is holy, and such are ye." (ASV).

Being disobedient to the word of God can cause the Spirit to be grieved. He is a person and your action or behavior will cause the spirit not to dwell in an unclean temple. Consider the story of Saul from 1 Samuel 16:14-15 *"¹⁴ Now the Spirit of Jehovah departed from Saul, and an evil spirit from Jehovah troubled him. ¹⁵ And Saul's servants said unto him, Behold now, an evil spirit from God troubleth thee."* (ASV). During this time the spirit came upon the men of God to empower. However, the same concept still applies. God will not allow His Spirit to live or come upon men that will not adhere to the standards of His Word. Paul tells the church at Ephesus: you cannot grieve the Holy Spirit and expect to be Holy. *"²⁹ Let no corrupt speech proceed out of your mouth, but such as is good for edifying as the need may be, that it may give grace to them that hear. ³⁰ And grieve not the Holy Spirit of God, in whom ye were sealed unto the day of redemption. ³¹ Let all bitterness, and wrath, and anger, and clamor, and railing, be put away from you, with all malice." (ASV).*

Preachers and teachers at all times should be Spirit-Led in their messages and not randomly preaching. God comes to His people with a purpose, therefore, the teacher should present with a purpose in mind. As a presenter to many people, the worst thing ever is to be boring to your audience; secondly, delivering a message that has no substance. Preachers and Teachers have to realize when their message is not impactful, despite their good intentions; however, whenever you speak it would be more persuasive to speak with authority. In Luke 4:31-37, when Christ was teaching in the synagogue in Capernaum, a city of Galilee. They were amazed how He spoke with authority and power. If Christians allow the Holy Spirit to operate without restriction, the power of the Holy Spirit will manifest itself through the gift God gave you. Ephesians provides

THE HOLY SPIRIT AND THE ANOINTING 53

an example of Paul's statement of spiritual Empowerment for understanding biblical text Ephesians 6:19.

Your message should be with life and power of the Holy Spirit speaking through you. Mark 1:21-22 gives the same account of Luke 4:31-37 but slightly different. Mark 1:21-22 says *"²¹ And they go into Capernaum; and straightway on the Sabbath day he entered into the synagogue and taught. ²² And they were astonished at his teaching: For he taught them as having authority, and not as the scribes"* (ASV). When souls come to the church, they should not leave the same way they came, if the anointing is flowing through the Christian. If only one soul is saved, the word of God has filled His purpose.

Christ gave the disciples power before He sent them out two-by-two Luke 9:1. *"And he called the twelve together, and gave them power and authority over all demons, and to cure diseases."* (ASV). If you have been truly called by Christ into the ministry, the *Empowerment* of the *Holy Spirit* should be manifested in your ministry.

What are the characteristics of being Spirit Empowered (having Authority)? Tony Sargent said it this way: *"It is the afflatus of the Spirit resting on the speaker. It is "power from on high." It is the preacher gliding on eagles' wings, soaring high, swooping low, carrying and being carried along by a dynamic other than his own. His consciousness of what is happening is not obliterated. He is not in a trance. He is being worked on but is aware that he is still working. He is being spoken through but he knows he is still speaking. The words are his but the facility with which they come compels him to realize that the source is beyond himself."* Tony Sargent, *The Sacred Anointing* (Wheaton, Ill.: Crossway, 1994, p29); (Greg Heisler, *Spirit-Led Preaching*: The Holy Spirit's Role in Sermon Preparation and Delivery, 2007, p138).

Often we have heard others say in similar terms, God has called me into the ministry or I think God is calling me into the ministry. If God is calling you into the ministry, then He has a purpose and a specific calling, and not all calling is a call to preach. *Preacher's call to preach is a call to study* God's word (Greg Heisler, p92). Paul tells Timothy to *study to show thyself approve unto God and not man* 2 Timothy 2:15.

These five elements describe the characteristics of Holy Spirit upon the preacher and they are not all exclusive to just these five:

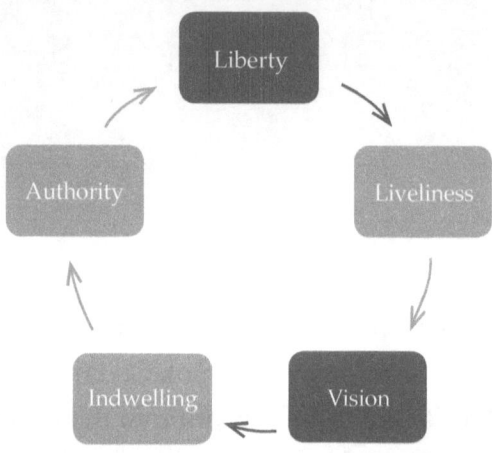

- Liberty or Freedom: we are at liberty to speak the introduction of the message and commence to exhort, but the Holy Spirit will give the empowerment to deliver the message in a more profound way through the spirit (anointing).

- Liveliness and Vitality: God's word is truth and life. God's word is made alive through spirit living within us. Hebrews 4:12 *"For the word of God is living and active, and sharper than any two-edged sword, and piercing even the dividing of soul and spirit, of both joints and marrow, and quick to discern the thoughts and intents of the heart"* (ASV). The preacher's sermon is made alive through the Holy Spirit.

- Vision and Dreams: Joel 2:29 and Acts 2:17 by the spirit of God. Proverbs 1:23 God will make known His word.

- Indwelling: the Holy Spirit takes possession of your life to live within you Romans 8:9, 1 Corinthians 3:16, Galatians 2:20, and Philippians 1:21.

- Authority and Power: 1 Corinthians 2:4-5.

Have you truly received the Gift of the Father, the "Holy Ghost" since you believe? The proof that you are a Christian is not found in the way you feel, but how you "obey" the Father, Christ and the Holy Spirit. If this becomes a question of debate within yourself, perhaps you may not be truly filled with the Spirit. Being filled with the Holy Spirit is a gift for all believers. Don't be surprised if this has not happened. There were many in Biblical days that didn't know if there were such a Spirit or even heard of the *Holy Spirit*. Acts 8:14-17. *"*[14]*Now when the apostles that were at Jerusalem heard that Samaria had received the word of God, they sent unto them Peter and John:* [15]*who, when they were come down, prayed for them, that they might receive the Holy Spirit:* [16]*for as yet it was fallen upon none of them: only they had been baptized into the name of the Lord Jesus.* [17]*Then laid they their hands on them, and they received the Holy Spirit"* (ASV). It is possible to acknowledge Christ and have a changed behavior, but it is very different when you are filled with the Holy Spirit.

No one can judge your salvation in Christ but you. It is your belief that a transformation has taken place within your heart and mind. When Paul was traveling through Ephesus, he came across disciples that had not received the Holy Spirit since they believed. It is possible today that there are Christians who have not received the baptism of the *Holy Spirit*. Acts 19:1-7 *"¹ And it came to pass, that, while Apollos was at Corinth, Paul having passed through the upper country came to Ephesus, and found certain disciples: ² and he said unto them, Did ye receive the Holy Spirit when ye believed? And they said unto him, Nay, we did not so much as hear whether the Holy Spirit was given. ³ And he said, Into what then were ye baptized? And they said, Into John's baptism. ⁴ And Paul said, John baptized with the baptism of repentance, saying unto the people that they should believe in him that should come after him, that is, in Jesus. ⁵ And when they heard this, they were baptized into the name of the Lord Jesus. ⁶ And when Paul had laid his hands upon them, the Holy Spirit came on them; and they spake with tongues, and prophesied. ⁷ And they were in all about twelve men"* (ASV).

You cannot be a preacher of Christ Gospel; and not teach or preach the Baptism of the *Holy Spirit* (*Holy Ghost*). It is essential for the sustaining of your ministry and strength for Christian living. I believe the church has become too complacent with the world view and not the *Holy Spirit* view. The Bible tells us not to be confirmed to this world Romans 12:2.

The Holy Spirit is the power for witnessing the true word of God; Christ's death, burial and resurrection; and He gives you the Authority in which Christian operates over Satan.

What role or purpose does the Holy Spirit have in the life of a believer? The *Holy Spirit* comes to teach the Christian or follower of Christ concerning the things of God and strengthens the church for ministry. He does not conform to *Spiritual Leaders* personal agenda, but only attends to the *Will of God* and *Christ*. Christians are the vessel in which God moves through and brings forth what He has planned for the people. The *Holy Spirit* as mentioned before comes to dwell in the believer's life to teach, guide and instruct him/her in the *Will of God*; and perfects the believer's gift for the glory of God and not self-glory.

The *Holy Spirit* sanctifies for service Romans 15:16, empowers for witnessing Acts 1:8, assists with prayer Romans 8:26, and helps Christians to live a Holy life Romans 8:5-16, Galatians 5:16. The Holy Spirit indwells 1 Corinthians 6:19, seals the Christians Ephesians 1:1-14, fills the believer Acts 2:4 and much more. Have you been truly filled by the *Holy Spirit* since you received the word of God in your heart?

Conclusion/Summary:

As teachers and preachers of the Gospel, and Christian, you must realize that we cannot *grieve* or *quench* the Holy Spirit that lives in us. When the Spirit is speaking through us it is not the time to be concerned about stepping on people's toes. You can *grieve* and *quench* the Holy Spirit many ways. Consider the teachings Paul stated in his writing to the church at Ephesians 4:30 *"And do not grieve the Holy Spirit of God, with whom you were sealed for the day of redemption."* and in 1 Thessalonians 5:19, *"Do not quench the Holy Spirit."* You can hinder the empowerment of the Holy Spirit in many ways:

- **Not prepared to deliver your message** — preacher, teachers and individuals are all obligated to study the word to be powerful in the demonstration of the spirit.

- **Nonprayer life** — will always hinder the work of the lord in your ministry. This is a daily guidance you need from the Holy Spirit. There are times when you have no words to say, but the Spirit makes intercession for us in prayer to God.

- **Lack of fasting** — is crucial in denying yourself to seek the will of God for your life, community, family, friends and the nations.

- **Fear of what man will say** — you cannot be a preacher or teacher of the Word of God being fearful of what man or congregation will say. The Holy Spirit will guide you through those troubled waters, but God didn't say you "**will not**" have them for the sake of the Gospel. Having authority comes with a price from the world and that is being criticized, talked about and more. Christ did nothing to the people of the world except preach the Gospel. And what happened to Him? The world crucified Him.

- **Living a sinful life** — in other words, rebellion against the structured living of a Christian. The Holy Spirit lives in a clean temple rather than an unclean temple. The mind is constantly at work battling thoughts that are against the nature and will of God.

- **A lack of faith/belief in the Gift of God** — God gave you the spiritual ability to perform but do you have the faith to allow the Holy Spirit to move through you? Your messages are only powerful when the Holy Spirit is at work in you.

- **Bad motives for the things you want** — Ask yourself this question: why are you preaching, teaching and speaking in the name of Christ? If this is not your true motive, then the Holy Spirit will not aid the ministry you think you're going to build. Christ and the Gospel are always first. Paul says 2 Corinthians 12:14 (NIV2011)

[14] *Now I am ready to visit you for the third time, and I will not be a burden to you, because what I want is not your possessions but you. After all, children should not have to save up for their parents, but parents for their children."* And Acts 24:16 (NIV2011), "[16] *So I strive always to keep my conscience clear before God and man."*

APPENDIX 1

A DEFINITION OF THE different types of Spiritual Gifts as outlined from the Amplified Study Bible, KJV topic on *Spiritual Gifts*, by Paul Walker, contributor to *Spiritual Answers to Hard Questions*. The gifts are separated into three sections: Gifts of the Father, Holy Spirit and Jesus Christ.

Romans 12:3-8: Gifts of the Father (Basic Life Purpose and Motivation)

1. PROPHECY
    a. To speak with forthrightness and insight, especially when enabled by the Spirit of God (Joel 2:28).
    b. To demonstrate moral boldness and uncompromising commitment to worthy values.
    c. To influence others in one's arena of influence with a positive spirit of social or spiritual righteousness.

2. MINISTRY
    a. To minister and render loving, general service to meet the needs of others.
    b. Illustrated in the work and office of the deacon. (Matthew 20:26).
3. TEACHING
    a. The supernatural ability to explain and apply the truths received from God for the church.
    b. Presupposes study and the Spirit's illumination providing the ability to make divine truth clear to the people.
    c. Considered distinct from the work of the prophet who speaks as the direct mouthpiece of God.
4. EXHORTATION
    a. Literal meaning is to call aside for the purpose of making an appeal.
    b. In a broader sense it means to entreat, comfort, or instruct (Acts 4:36; Heb. 10:25).
5. GIVING
    a. The essential meaning is to give out of a spirit of generosity.
    b. In a more technical sense it refers to those with resources aiding those without such resources (2 Cor. 8:2; 9:11-13).
    c. This gift is to be exercised liberally without outward show or pride. (2 Cor. 1:12; 8:2; 9:11. 13.

6. LEADERSHIP
    a. Refers to the one "standing in front."
    b. Involves the exercise of the Holy Spirit in modeling, superintending and developing the body of Christ.
    c. Leadership is to be exercised with diligence.
7. MERCY
    a. To feel sympathy with the misery of another.
    b. To relate to others in empathy, respect and honesty.
    c. To be effective, this gift is to be exercised with kindness and cheerfulness — not as a matter of duty.

1 Corinthians 12:8-10, 28: Gifts of the Holy Spirit

1. WORD OF WISDOM
    a. Supernatural perspective to ascertain the divine means for accomplishing God's will in given situations.
    b. Divinely given power to appropriate spiritual intuition in problem solving
    c. Sense of divine direction
    d. Being led by the Holy Spirit to act appropriately in a given set of circumstances.
    e. Knowledge rightly applied: wisdom works interactively with knowledge and discernment.
2. WORD OF KNOWLEDGE
    a. Supernatural revelation of the divine will and plan.

b. Supernatural insight or understanding of circumstances or a body of facts by revelation: that is, without assistance of any human resources but solely by divine aid.
   c. Implies a deeper and more advanced understanding of the communicated acts of God.
   d. Involves moral wisdom for right living and relationships.
   e. Requires objective understanding concerning divine things in human duties.
   f. May also refer to knowledge of God of the things that belongs to God, as related in the gospel.

3. **FAITH**
   a. The ability to believe God without doubt.
   b. The ability to combat unbelief.
   c. The ability to meet adverse circumstances with trust in God's messages and words.

4. **GIFTS OF HEALINGS**
   a. Refers to supernatural healing without aid.
   b. May include divinely assisted application of human instrumentation and medical means of treatment.
   c. Does not discount the use of God's creative gifts.

5. **WORKING OF MIRACLES**
   a. Supernatural power to intervene and counteract earthly and evil forces.
   b. Literally means a display of power giving the ability to go beyond the natural.

c. Operates closely with the gifts of faith and healing to bring authority over sin, Satan, sickness and the binding forces of this age.
6. PROPHECY
   a. Divinely inspired and anointed utterance.
   b. Supernatural proclamation in a known language.
   c. May be possessed and operated by all who have the indwelling of the Holy Spirit (1 Cor. 14:30).
   d. Intellect, faith and will are operative in this gift, but its exercise is not intellectually based. It is calling forth words from the Spirit of God.
7. DISCERNING OF SPIRITS
   a. The power to detect the realm of spirits and their activities.
   b. Implies the power of spiritual insight: supernatural revelation of plans and purpose of the Enemy and his forces.
8. DIFFERENT KINDS OF TONGUES
   a. Supernatural utterance in languages not known to the speaker; these languages may be existent in the world, revived from some past culture, or "unknown" in the sense that they are a means of communication inspired by the Holy Spirit (Is. 288:11; Mark 16:17; Acts 2:1; 10:44-48; 19:1-7; 1 Cor. 12:10, 28-31; 13:1-3; 14:2, 4-22, 26-32).

b. Serve as an evidence and sign of the indwelling and working of the Holy Spirit.

9. INTERPRETATION OF TONGUES
    a. The power to reveal the meaning of tongues spoken.
    b. Functions not as an operation of the mind of man but as the mind of the Holy Spirit.
    c. Is exercised as a miraculous and supernatural phenomenon as are the gift of speaking in tongues and the gift of prophecy.

Ephesians 1:11 (Also 1 Cor. 12:28): Gifts of the Son (to facilitate and equip the body of the church)

1. APOSTLES
    a. In apostolic days referred to a select group chosen to directly carry out the ministry of Christ; included the assigned task given to a few to complete the sacred canon of the Holy Scriptures.
    b. Implies the exercise of a distinct representative role of broader leadership given by Christ.
    c. Functions as a messenger or spokesman of God.
    d. In contemporary times refers to those who have the spirit of apostleship and remarkably extended the work of the church, opening fields to the gospel and overseeing larger sections of the body of Jesus Christ.

2. PROPHET
    a. A spiritually mature spokesman/proclaimer with a special, divinely-focused message to the church or the world.
    b. A person uniquely gifted at times with insight into future events.
3. EVANGELIST
    a. Refers primarily to a special gift of preaching or witnessing in a way that brings unbelievers into the experience of salvation.
    b. The gift of the evangelist operates for the establishment of new works, while pastors and teachers follow up to organize and sustain.
    c. Essentially, the gift of the evangelist operates to establish converts and to gather them spiritually and literally into the body of Christ.
4. PASTOR/TEACHER
    a. The word "pastor" comes from a root meaning "to protect," from which we get the word "shepherd."
    b. Implies the function of a shepherd/leader to nurture, teach and care for the spiritual needs of the body.
5. MISSIONARY (some think of "apostle" or "evangelist" as missionary workers).
    a. Implies the unfolding of a plan for making the gospel known to the entire world (Rom 1:16).

b. Illustrates an attitude of humility necessary for receiving a call to remote areas and unknown situations (Is. 6:1-13).
   c. Connotes an inner compulsion to lead the world to an understanding of Jesus Christ (2 Cor. 5:14-20).

Special Gifts
1. HOSPITALITY
   a. Literally means to love, to do or to do with pleasure.
   b. Illustrates Peter's notion of one of the two categories of gifts: 1) teaching, 2) practical service (1 Peter 4:10, 11).
   c. Was utilized in caring for believers and workers who visited to worship, work and become involved in the body of Christ.
   d. Illustrated in the teaching of Jesus concerning judgment (Matthew 25:35, 40).
2. CELIBACY (Matthew 19:10; 1 Cor. 7:7-9, 27; 1 Timothy 4:3; Rev. 14:4).
   a. The Bible considers marriage to be honorable, ordained of God and a need for every person.
   b. Implies a special gift of celibacy, which frees the individual from the duties, pressure and preoccupations of family life, allowing undivided attention to the Lord's work.

3. MARTYRDOM (1 Peter 4:12,13)
    a. Illustrated in the Spirit of Stephen (Acts 7:59, 60).
    b. Fulfilled in the attitude of Paul (2 Timothy 4:6-8).

Scripture: Romans 8:16-17

You are Sons and Daughters of God.

Scripture: 2 Corinthians 5:17

You are a New Person in Christ Jesus.

Growing Spiritually through Prayer and God's Word
The very essence of our life is to be spiritually connected to God and Christ. The relationship you have with Christ depends primarily upon your devotion to study and prayer. We as Christians must have a consistent prayer life and

BIBLIOGRAPHY

H. Franklin Paschall, Herschel H. Hobbs. (1972). *Teacher's Bible Commentary.* Nashville, TN: B&H Publishing Group.

Henry T. Blackaby and Richard Blackaby. (2011). *Spiritual Leadership.* Nashville, TN: B&H Publishing Group.

Holman Illustrated Bible Dictionary

Iorg, J. (2007). *The Character of Leadership.* Database Wordsearch Corp.

Jack W. Hayford Litt. D, Sam Middleton, D. Min; Jerry Horner, ThD. (1991). *Spirit Filled Life Bible.* (J. Hayford, Ed.) Nashville, TN: Thomas Nelson.

John F. Walvoord, Roy B. Zuck. (1985). *The Bible Knowledge Commentary.* Canada, England, USA: Scripture Press Publications, Inc.

Sanders, J. O. (2007). *Spiritual Leadership, Principles of Excellence for Every Believer.* Database Wordsearch Corp.

ABOUT THE AUTHOR

FREDERICK COFFEY was born in Florence, Alabama to Isaiah and Madelyn Coffey. He is the last of ten siblings and he has 6 children of his own, now adults. He grew up primarily Baptist as a member Tabernacle Missionary Baptist Church, Florence, AL. He joined the U.S. Army at 17 and served our country for 22 years. He had the privilege of learning from some great pastors and missionaries who impacted his life strongly: Dr. Lennon Trawick, Bishop A. LaDell Thomas, Sr., Dr. Donald Smith, Pastor Terry Whitley and Missionary Lillian Billie. Frederick Coffey taught Sunday School and was President of the Brotherhood Ministry under Dr. Lennon Trawick, Full Gospel Holiness COGIC, Budingen, Germany. In 1990, he became a Licensed Minister by Bishop A. L. Thomas, Sr. of Texas Southeast II Ecclesiastic Jurisdiction.

In 1999, he was ordained as Elder by Bishop Thomas Sr., and appointed pastor of Tate Memorial COGIC. He served as President of Youth Service (YPWW) under Bishop Thomas Sr., and Pastor of Camp Red Cloud COGIC, Korea. During Desert Shield and Desert Storm, Frederick, along with another minister, held tent services and revivals in the deserts of Kuwait during deployments.

Education: Frederick has completed two Masters Degrees, Human Resource Management and an MBA in Business Administration; BS in Administration and Management; He is certified in Kiazen Process Improvement. Now, he is completing his third Masters in Christian Studies and will pursue a Doctorate in Christian Leadership or Ministry to share the knowledge and wisdom with others. His inspiration to return to seminary school was inspired by Pastor Terry Whitley. "Frederick, if you desire to become a pastor again and have a passion for the gospel and people, I suggest you obtain an education in ministry." Frederick has challenged himself to complete his mentor instruction and will complete his Masters in Christian Studies august 2015. He will begin his Doctorate spring of 2016.

Most people from Florence, Alabama know who I am. Many of them are very familiar with the Coffey family, because of my parents or myself active in the sport of basketball at Coffee High School. Even then, many did not really know things I went through in life for many years. I know what it is like to live with a secret and not tell anyone until you build up courage to face the fact it will change what happened. What you're about to read is true; and I only shared this incident with three people; my sister Deborah, Bishop A. LaDell Thomas Sr., and my Pastor, Terry Whitley.

Around the age of 9 or 11, a close friend of the family molested me. I never told anyone, not even my spouse. Until now, only three people actually knew the story and they are mentioned above. Now, to everyone who knows me, this is a revelation, even my childhood friends who I kept it a secret from all these years. What hurts the most now is, I never told my father and mother, allowing them the opportunity to protect me, my brothers and sisters (except Deborah), nor my own children, because of the shame I felt. Mainly I kept this to myself to avoid being labeled as something that I am not. As a child living in fear of what the friend of the family said he would do, I lived with these emotions and feelings of guilt all of my life. *Forgiveness is only a word if it cannot be demonstrated in the heart and lived out within the life of a Christian.* Today, I can stand before God, and the man, and honestly say in my heart, I forgive you and pray that God has delivered your mind and body from an unclean spirit. You have to wait until **Book II** to engage more into the insight on forgiveness.

Secondly, it's not easy to believe God has a plan for everything; especially when, just as an expectation arrives, it's gone. As a man who doesn't show his emotions easily — I was hurt by the death of my young daughter, Laura Yvette Coffey.

Sometimes, there is no "Why" or "Answer" from God, only silence.

As a parent I know what it's like to experience the incarceration of a child, and having to deal with the mixed emotions of divorce.

You analyze everything in your past to determine where you went wrong or what you could have done differently to prevent either of these situations from coming to fruition.

Then, from that point the feeling of guilt and embarrassment makes you feel unworthy to teach or preach the Gospel. The process of "healing" is never easy.

However, I learned that, for me, surrendering my past to God has been the greatest peace I've ever experienced.

People are going to prejudge and criticize you about your past and your failures, but what matters most to me is the transformation and change that has brought me to who I am now in Christ.

www.ingramcontent.com/pod-product-compliance
Lightning Source LLC
Chambersburg PA
CBHW031427290426
44110CB00011B/552